WILLIAM SHAKESPEARE

Robin Johnson

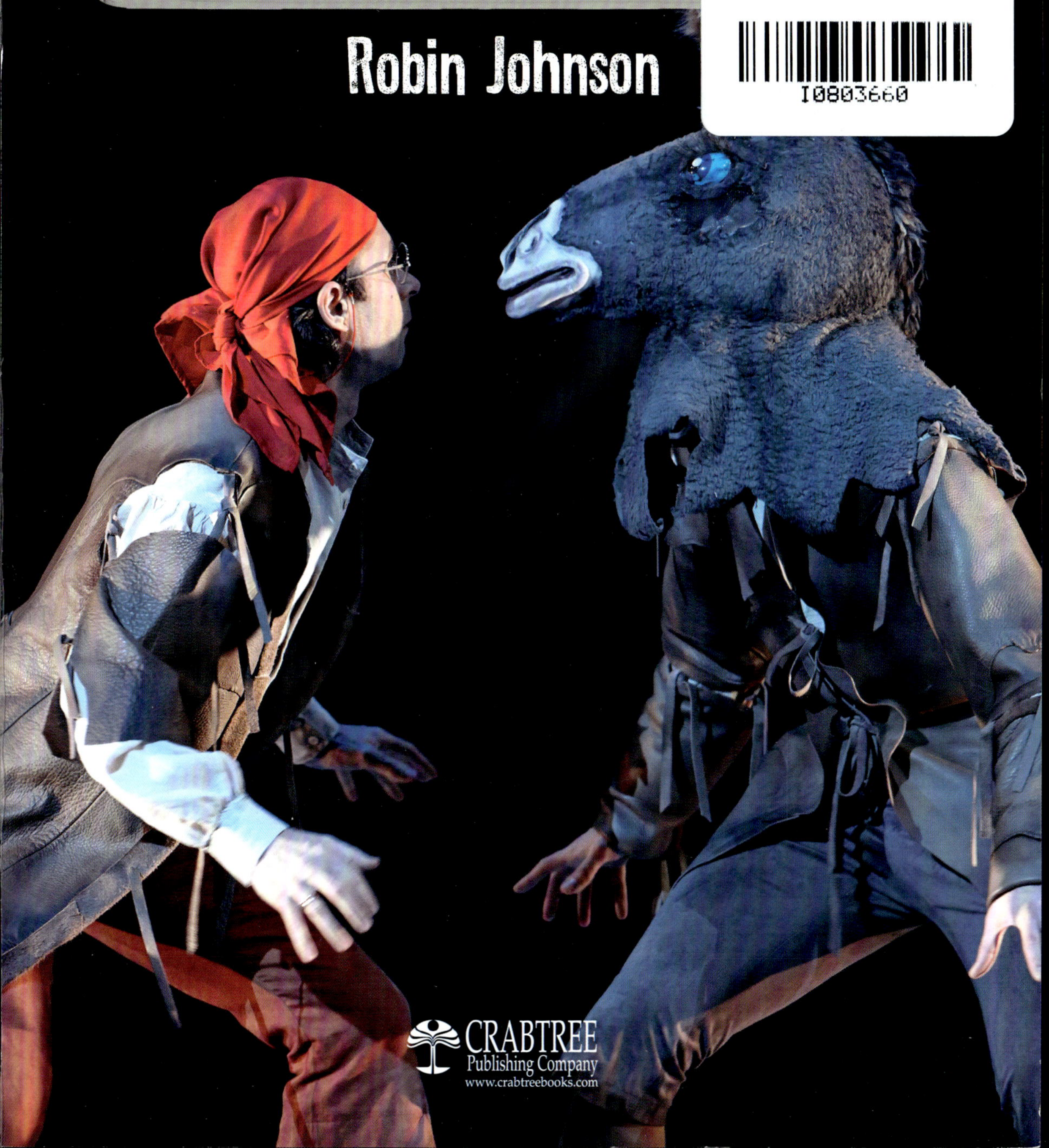

CRABTREE
Publishing Company
www.crabtreebooks.com

Crabtree Publishing Company
www.crabtreebooks.com

Author: Robin Johnson
Publishing plan research and development: Reagan Miller
Project coordinator: Crystal Sikkens
Editors: Sonya Newland, Crystal Sikkens
Proofreader: Janine Deschenes
Original design: Tim Mayer (Mayer Media)
Book design: Clare Nicholas
Cover design: Ken Wright
Map: Stefan Chabluk
Production coordinator and prepress technician: Ken Wright
Print coordinator: Margaret Amy Salter
Production coordinated by: White-Thomson Publishing

Photographs:
Alamy: North Wind Picture Archives: p. 8; Moviestore collection Ltd: pp. 22–23; dieKleinert: p. 25; The Print Collector: pp. 34–35; Bridgeman Art Library: McBride, Angus (1931-2007) / Private Collection / © Look and Learn: p. 40; Corbis: National Geographic Creative: p. 9; © Philcold/Dreamstime: cover; Stefano Bianchetti: pp. 10–11, 38–39; Roger Wood: pp. 16–17; Araldo de Luca: p. 18; Bettmann: p. 37; HO/Reuters: p. 42; Getty Images: Universal History Archive: p. 27; iStock: ZU_09: p. 12; Craig McCausland: p. 14; treeffe: p. 21; Ary6: p. 29; Shutterstock: meirion Matthias: pp. 1, 44–45; Iakov Kalinin: pp. 3, 30–31; nito: pp. 7, 36; Everett Historical: p. 15; Bildagentur Zoonar GmbH: p. 17; R.A.R. de Bruijn Holding BV: p. 20; stemack: p. 24; diak: pp. 28–29; Georgy Kuryatov: pp. 32–33; konstantinks: p. 41; riekephotos: p. 43; Wikimedia: cover, 26; Jean-Leon_Gerome_Pollice_Verso: pp. 4–5; Marie-Lan Nguyen: p. 13; Jastrow: p. 19.

Library and Archives Canada Cataloguing in Publication

Johnson, Robin (Robin R.), author
William Shakespeare / Robin Johnson.

(Crabtree chrome)
Includes index.
Issued in print and electronic formats.
ISBN 978-0-7787-2290-8 (bound).--ISBN 978-0-7787-2229-8 (paperback).--ISBN 978-1-4271-8087-2 (html)

1. Shakespeare, William, 1564-1616--Juvenile literature. 2. Dramatists, English--Early modern, 1500-1700--Biography--Juvenile literature. I. Title. II. Series: Crabtree chrome

PR2895.J65 2016 j822.3'3 C2015-907945-4
C2015-907946-2

Library of Congress Cataloging-in-Publication Data

CIP available at Library of Congress

Crabtree Publishing Company

www.crabtreebooks.com 1-800-387-7650

Printed in Canada/022016/MA20151130

In Canada: We acknowledge the financial support of the Government of Canada through the Canada Book Fund for our publishing activities.

Published in Canada
Crabtree Publishing
616 Welland Ave.
St. Catharines, ON
L2M 5V6

Published in the United States
Crabtree Publishing
PMB 59051
350 Fifth Avenue, 59th Floor
New York, New York 10118

Published in the United Kingdom
Crabtree Publishing
Maritime House
Basin Road North, Hove
BN41 1WR

Published in Australia
Crabtree Publishing
3 Charles Street
Coburg North
VIC 3058

Contents

Much Ado About Nothing?	4
The Life and Times of Shakespeare	8
Shakespeare's Work	16
Renaissance Men	28
All's Well That Ends Well	34
Learning More	46
Glossary	47
Index	48

Much Ado About Nothing?

William the Great

William Shakespeare is called the greatest English writer of all time. Students read his work in classrooms everywhere. His plays are performed on stages and screens around the globe. But is Shakespeare really that great? Or is it much **ado** about nothing?

▶ *Shakespeare is one of the most famous writers in the world.*

No Great Shakes?

Shakespeare lived about 400 years ago. He used a quill dipped in ink to write his plays and poems. He used language that sounds old and strange to us today. So why should we bother reading his work? Does Shakespeare still matter?

What's in a name? Shakespeare is called "The Bard" and "The Swan of Avon." A bard is a poet. Avon is the town where he grew up.

▼ *In Shakespeare's time, people wrote everything by hand. They used large feathers, called quills, as pens.*

ado: fuss or foolish talk

The Role of a Lifetime

Shakespeare lived long ago, so little is known about him. We do know that he played many parts in his time, however. He was a husband and a father. He was a poet, an actor, and a successful businessman. But he is most famous for being a **playwright**.

"All the world's a stage,
And all the men and women merely players;
They have their exits and their entrances;
And one man in his time plays many parts..."

William Shakespeare, *As You Like It*. In this passage, Shakespeare compares the world to a stage. He says that people are like actors in a play. During their lives, they play many parts.

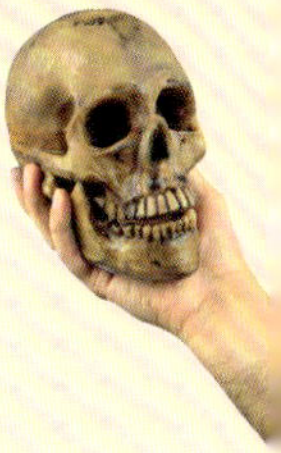

A Man of Many Words

Shakespeare's work speaks for itself—and it speaks volumes! He wrote at least 38 plays. He also wrote more than 150 poems. There were many other great writers at the time, so what separates Shakespeare's work from theirs? Why has he stood the test of time?

▲ *This painting shows characters from some of Shakespeare's plays. He told many tales, but he did not write his own life story. Today, we know little about him.*

playwright: someone who writes plays

The Life and Times of Shakespeare

A Star Is Born

Shakespeare was born around April 23, 1564, in a small market town northwest of London, England called Stratford-upon-Avon. Shakespeare's father, John, was a successful glove-maker and businessman. He was also important in local government. Shakespeare's mother, Mary, came from a wealthy farming family with a high place in society.

▼ *This is the house where Shakespeare was born. Today, it is a museum.*

The Oldest Son

John and Mary had eight children, but their first two daughters did not survive. Growing up, William was the oldest child in the family. He had three younger brothers, named Gilbert, Richard, and Edmund. He also had two sisters, Anne and Joan. Anne died when she was just seven years old. At the time, children often caught deadly diseases that had no cure.

▶ *This map shows the location of Stratford-upon-Avon in England, where Shakespeare was born.*

Shakespeare was born during the English Renaissance. This was a time of great change and growth in England. Long and bloody wars had ended. There was new interest in science and **literature**. Many great works of art were created during this period.

literature: written works that are considered very good or important

Shakespeare in School

Shakespeare probably started school at the age of six or seven. He may have studied Latin and read stories from **ancient** times. Latin is an old language that was used by the Romans long ago. Students also learned how to memorize lines and act in plays—skills that would come in handy for Shakespeare.

▼ *In Shakespeare's time, boys from wealthier families went to grammar school to learn how to read and write.*

England got its first printing press in 1476. The new invention allowed people to make books quickly and cheaply. Students like Shakespeare had access to textbooks and ancient literature that was not available before.

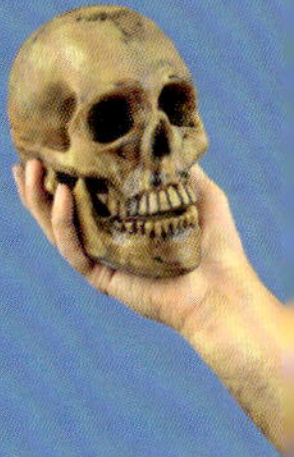

Shakespeare in Love

Shakespeare left school around the age of 15. His father had money troubles and Shakespeare probably had to work to help support the family. No one knows how he spent his next few years. In 1582, at the age of 18, Shakespeare married a 26-year-old woman named Anne Hathaway. Together, they had three children—a girl named Susanna and twins called Hamnet and Judith.

▼ *The home where Anne Hathaway lived as a child still stands in Warwickshire, England, about 1 mile (1.6 km) from Stratford-upon-Avon.*

ancient: very old

First Act

In the mid-1580s, Shakespeare set out for London to find work in the theater. London was a big, busy city that was full of shops, inns, palaces, and theaters. People came to the city to find their fortunes. They gathered in public playhouses to watch the latest shows. Shakespeare got his big break in London—probably as an actor. But soon he was writing plays, too.

▲ *Shakespeare's wife Anne was left alone in Stratford-upon-Avon to raise their children.*

Making History

Shakespeare made history with *Henry VI*. Between 1589 and 1591, he wrote three plays about the former king of England. The plays brought the king's **reign** and wars to life. They also showed the talents of the up-and-coming writer. By 1592, Shakespeare's plays had hit the London stage. The young playwright was on his way.

Queen Elizabeth I ruled England from 1558 to 1603. She was a smart, fair, and popular monarch. During her long reign, the country was strong and mostly peaceful. It was a golden age in English history that became known as the Elizabethan era.

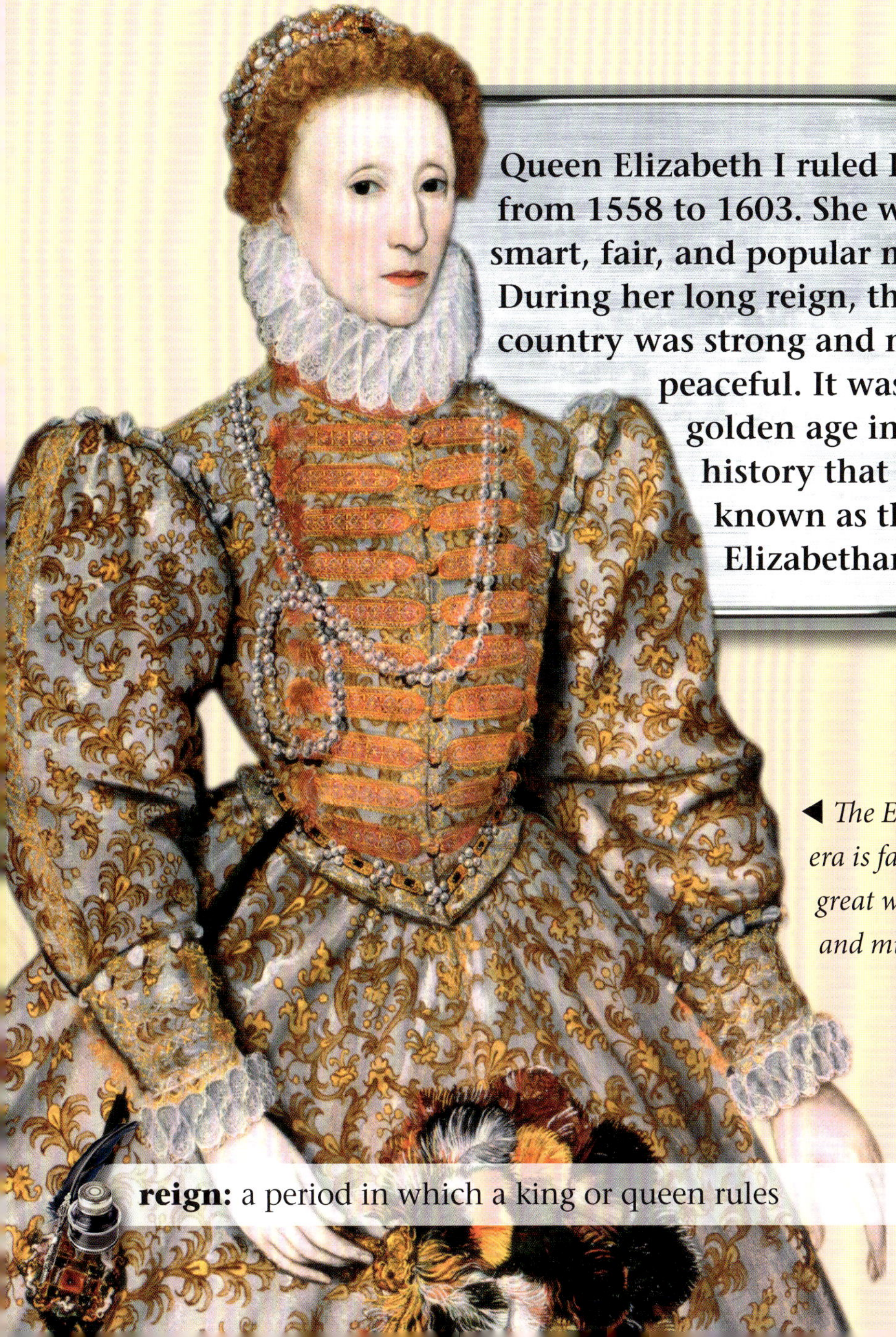

◀ *The Elizabethan era is famous for great writers and musicians.*

reign: a period in which a king or queen rules

The Company He Kept

In 1594, Shakespeare joined a company of actors called the Lord Chamberlain's Men. The men performed in a playhouse outside London called The Theatre. Shakespeare likely started out on stage, but his true talents took him behind the scenes. He wrote a play called *A Midsummer Night's Dream*. Then he wrote *Romeo and Juliet*. Before long, Shakespeare was writing most of the company's plays.

Playing for Keeps

Shakespeare spent the rest of his career with the playing company. He wrote plays and had small acting roles on stage. He also owned part of the company. A group of men, called sharers, split the costs and any money made from the shows. Shakespeare and the other sharers grew wealthy. In 1599, they built a large playhouse in London called the Globe.

◄ *The Globe was a three-story, open-air* ***amphitheater*** *that held as many as 3,000 people.*

Shakespeare's playing company was named for the Lord Chamberlain, a wealthy Englishman and cousin of Queen Elizabeth I. When King James came to the throne in 1603, the company was renamed the King's Men.

amphitheater: a round building with layers of seats around a stage

The Comedies

Many of Shakespeare's early plays were comedies. They were funny stories with silly characters and unlikely plot twists. They had mix-ups, marriages, and happy endings. They were just what the people of London needed at the time. In the 1590s, the **bubonic plague** was sweeping through England. People flocked to theaters to boost their spirits and forget their cares for a while.

◀ *Plague doctors wore special masks so they did not catch the deadly disease.*

During the time of the bubonic plague, the city of London was crowded and dirty. This caused diseases to spread quickly. Thousands of people died painful, bloody deaths from the plague. At least one of Shakespeare's sisters died of the disease.

A Master of Disguise

Shakespeare's comic characters often dress up and play tricks on others. Men disguise themselves as women. Women disguise themselves as men. In the Elizabethan era, male actors played all the parts in plays—even the roles of women. In some plays, men would play the parts of women who were trying to disguise themselves as men!

▼ *In* A Midsummer Night's Dream, *one of the characters is turned into a donkey!*

bubonic plague: a deadly disease spread by fleas

The Poems

In 1593, London theaters were closed because of the plague. So Shakespeare published narrative poems instead of plays that year. A narrative poem has characters and tells a story. In "Venus and Adonis," a Roman goddess chases a young man—who dies chasing a boar. In "The Rape of Lucrece," the son of a Roman king abuses a woman who is pure and beautiful.

▲ *The poem "Venus and Adonis" describes the relationship between a goddess and a handsome young human.*

Shakespeare's Sonnets

Shakespeare also wrote sonnets—154 of them! A sonnet is a poem with 14 lines. Each line has 10 **syllables** and rhymes with another line. Shakespeare packed some big subjects into his short poems. He wrote about love, time, beauty, death, and other topics. In his most famous sonnet, he compares his true love to a summer day.

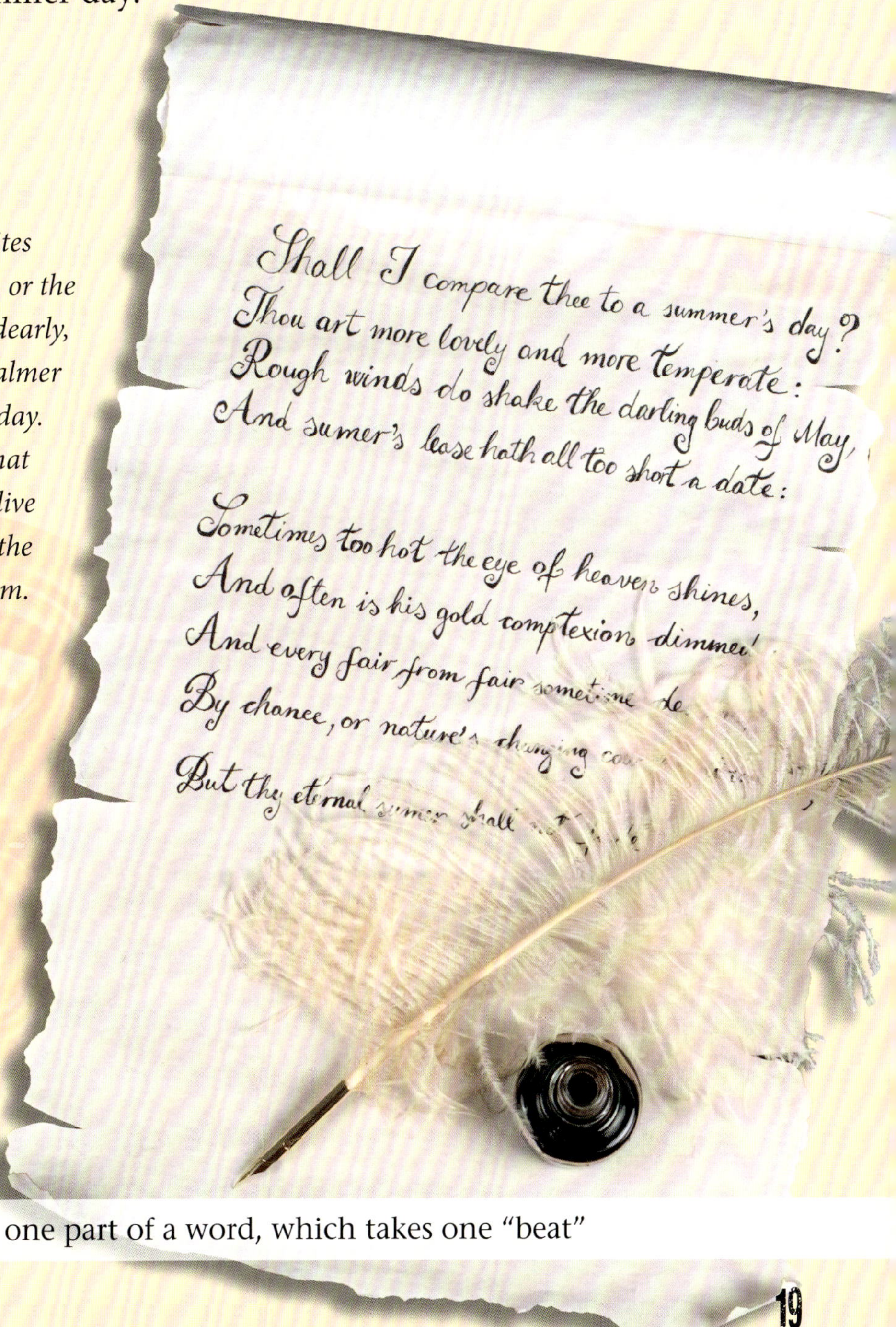

▶ *In Sonnet 18, Shakespeare writes that his beloved, or the person he loves dearly, is prettier and calmer than a summer day. He also writes that his beloved will live forever through the words of the poem.*

syllable: one part of a word, which takes one "beat"

The Histories

When the London theaters reopened, audiences went to see Shakespeare's history plays. Because writers at the time had history books to read, Shakespeare's histories are based on facts about real rulers and their battles. They are still products of Shakespeare's imagination, however. He created colorful characters and added dramatic details to entertain the crowds.

▲ *In December 1594, Shakespeare performed his play* The Two Gentlemen of Verona *for the queen at her palace.*

God Save the Queen

Shakespeare's early histories also had to please the queen. Queen Elizabeth I was the fifth and last ruler of the Tudor **dynasty**. Shakespeare painted her ancestor, King Henry VI, as a peaceful, saintly man, even though the real Henry VI had gone mad. He showed Richard III—the last ruler of the opposing York dynasty—as an ugly, evil hunchback.

Queen Elizabeth I enjoyed watching plays, but she could not go to rowdy public theaters. So Shakespeare took the shows to her. He performed at the royal palace in 1594 and 1597.

dynasty: a line of rulers from a particular family

The Tragedies

Shakespeare's **tragedies** were the most popular plays in Renaissance England. They brought audiences to tears, and people still came back for more! The tragedies feature main characters with fatal flaws, such as greed or pride. The faults lead the characters to their downfall and their death.

▼ Macbeth *is a tragic tale of witchcraft, murder, and madness.*

Tragic Heroes

Shakespeare created some of the greatest tragic heroes ever written. Macbeth is a greedy general whose thirst for power earns him the throne—and a bloody death. King Lear is a foolish old ruler who gives his kingdom to his two evil daughters instead of his good, fair daughter. Hamlet is a prince who seeks revenge for his father's murder, but ends up dead himself.

▼ *King Lear goes mad after he realizes the mistake he made by giving the kingdom to his two evil daughters.*

Shakespeare had tragic times in his own life. His only son, Hamnet, died at the age of 11. *Hamlet* and other tragedies may have been shaped by the young boy's death.

tragedies: stories with sad events and unhappy endings

Star-Crossed Lovers

Some of Shakespeare's greatest tragedies are love stories. They are sweet, sad tales of star-crossed lovers. Star-crossed means the lovers are doomed by the heavens to fail. The tragic couples in Shakespeare's plays are torn apart by families, wars, and other outside forces. They fight to the death for their true love.

> **"The course of true love never did run smooth."**
>
> William Shakespeare

O Romeo, Romeo!

Shakespeare's *Romeo and Juliet* is one of the most famous love stories ever written. It is the tale of a young couple forced apart by their **feuding** families. Romeo and Juliet meet at a costume party and fall deeply in love. They marry in secret. But then the plot twists and turns and things go horribly wrong. Both Romeo and Juliet die in the end.

▲ *The balcony scene in* Romeo and Juliet *is one of the most famous moments in literature.*

feuding: long, bitter fighting between families

The Romances

Shakespeare made magic with his final plays. They are called **romances** or tragicomedies. These plays mix humor and tragedy together. They have sad scenes, magic moments, and mostly happy endings. King James I preferred this type of play—so Shakespeare gave him what he wanted.

▲ *The characters in* The Tempest *experience confusion and danger, but the play has a happy ending.*

***The Two Noble Kinsmen* was Shakespeare's final play. He wrote the tragicomedy with a playwright named John Fletcher around 1613.**

Something Special

Shakespeare's playing company used special effects to bring romances and other plays to life. Actors hung from the theater roof on ropes and wires. They sprung up through trap doors in the stage floor. Fireworks exploded and cannons were fired. Spirits appeared and storms raged on stage.

▼ *In modern productions, directors of Shakespeare's plays still use special effects to show things such as storms.*

romances: stories that blend comedy, tragedy, and magic

Will Power

Shakespeare's plays were hits. He became famous in the London theater world. His name was added to posters to bring crowds to the shows. Fans flocked to the Globe theater to see his latest plays. Business was booming and Shakespeare became wealthy. He used his earnings to buy land and a large brick house, called New Place, in Stratford-upon-Avon.

▲ *The house at New Place was torn down in 1759, but visitors can still walk through the gardens on the grounds of Shakespeare's last home.*

Bad Press

Not everyone praised Shakespeare at the time, however. Some scorned him because he did not have a university education. Some felt he was not as talented as other great writers at the time. An English author named Robert Greene publicly insulted Shakespeare. He called him an "**upstart** crow" that used the feathers of other birds to make himself look better.

Shakespeare's new home was the second-biggest house in Stratford-upon-Avon. It had ten fireplaces, two barns, and an orchard.

upstart: rising to power or fame quickly

The Others

Shakespeare was not the only talented writer in Renaissance England. It was a golden age of literature. Christopher Marlowe was born the same year as Shakespeare. He wrote tragic plays—until he died a tragic death himself at the age of 29. Ben Jonson wrote popular satires for the stage. Satires are stories that use humor to show a character's faults. There were many great playwrights at the time, but none were quite like Shakespeare.

▼ *Shakespeare wrote far more than any other playwright at the time. This painting represents many of his works.*

"Soule of the Age! The applause! delight! The wonder of our stage!"

English playwright Ben Jonson, describing Shakespeare

◀ *Even Shakespeare's darkest tragedies often had comic moments. Here, Hamlet holds the skull of a poor man named Yorick in a funny scene.*

Not Like the Others

Unlike other writers at the time, Shakespeare wrote all types of plays. He mixed types in new ways. His comedies have sad moments. His tragedies have comic scenes. Shakespeare explored new subjects and twisted plots in creative ways. His characters are colorful and well developed. They act like real people, who helpfully show their true feelings in **soliloquies**.

soliloquies: speeches that show the thoughts of lone characters

▼ *Some experts argue that Shakespeare's shaky signature proves he was not educated enough to have become a master playwright.*

Too Good to Be True?

Was William Shakespeare too good to be true? He was the son of a glove-maker from a small English town. He had little education or **opportunity** after his father lost his money. How did a man with simple beginnings rise to such greatness? Why do we know so little about his life? And how could one person alone write so many plays? For some people, it seemed like too much of a good thing. Someone must have helped him!

Could It Be True?

Long after Shakespeare's death, people began to claim he did not write all his own work. They believed he worked closely with Christopher Marlowe or other playwrights. Others claimed that Shakespeare did not write anything at all! They believed Sir Francis Bacon or other great thinkers published their work in his name. The men may have hidden their names to avoid trouble with the throne. Most people do not agree with these theories, however.

▶ *Sir Francis Bacon had a high position in England's government. He worked closely with King James I.*

Sir Francis Bacon was a noted scientist and a great thinker. He believed that scientists should use experiments to prove their ideas. If Bacon were still alive during these claims, he would have demanded proof that he wrote Shakespeare's plays!

opportunity: a good chance to succeed

All's Well That Ends Well

Parting Is Such Sweet Sorrow

William Shakespeare died on April 23, 1616, at the age of 52. The cause of his death is unknown. When Shakespeare died, only about half of his plays had been published. They were printed in small books called quartos. The first complete collection of Shakespeare's work was published in 1623, seven years after his death. It is called the First Folio.

◀ *The First Folio sold well and was reprinted again and again.*

Alive and Well

Shakespeare lived and wrote a long time ago. The language he used sounds very different from how we speak today. But Shakespeare's poems and plays are still **relevant**. We can relate to the subjects, plots, and characters in his work. We quote the lines he wrote and use the words he created. The Bard continues to entertain audiences and shape the work of today's writers.

When Shakespeare died, he left his wife his "second-best bed." It sounds insulting, but it was probably the bed they shared in their home. The best bed would have been saved for guests and passed down to his children.

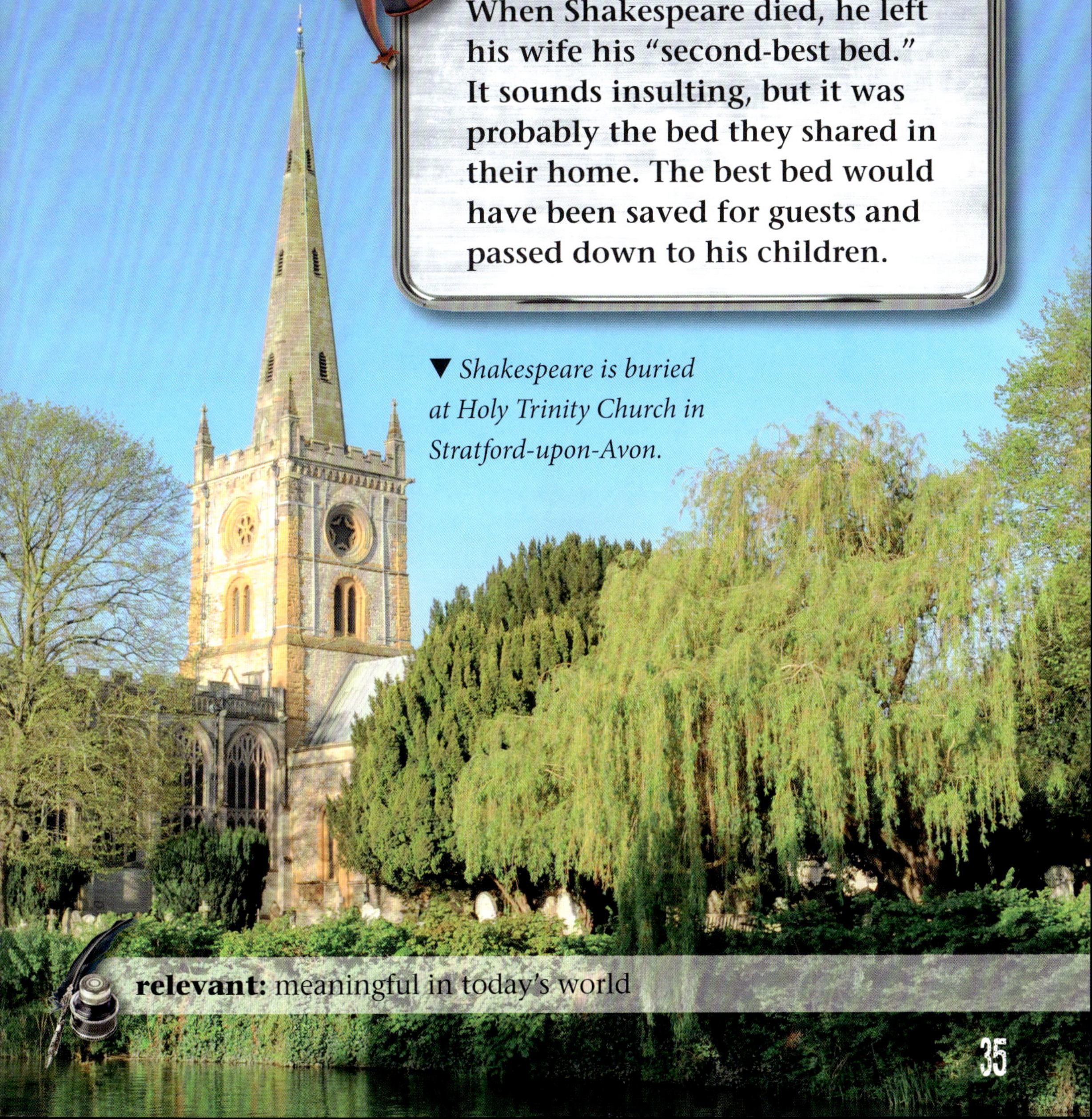

▼ *Shakespeare is buried at Holy Trinity Church in Stratford-upon-Avon.*

relevant: meaningful in today's world

Timeless Themes

Certain **themes** show up in Shakespeare's work time and time again. He showed that things are not always as they seem. Mighty characters fall because they have human flaws. Some couples are doomed from the start. People can change over time. These themes are still common in books, plays, movies, and television shows today.

Lots of Plots

Many modern stories follow plots used by Shakespeare. Couples are torn apart by rival gangs or feuding families. Greedy people do terrible deeds to grab power and stay in control. Crafty characters pretend to be others or fake their own deaths. Shakespeare's plots brought fans to the Globe, and still bring us to theaters today.

Shakespeare did not invent all the themes and plots he used. In fact, many of his plays are based on the work of other authors. But Shakespeare told the stories in new ways and made them more popular than ever before.

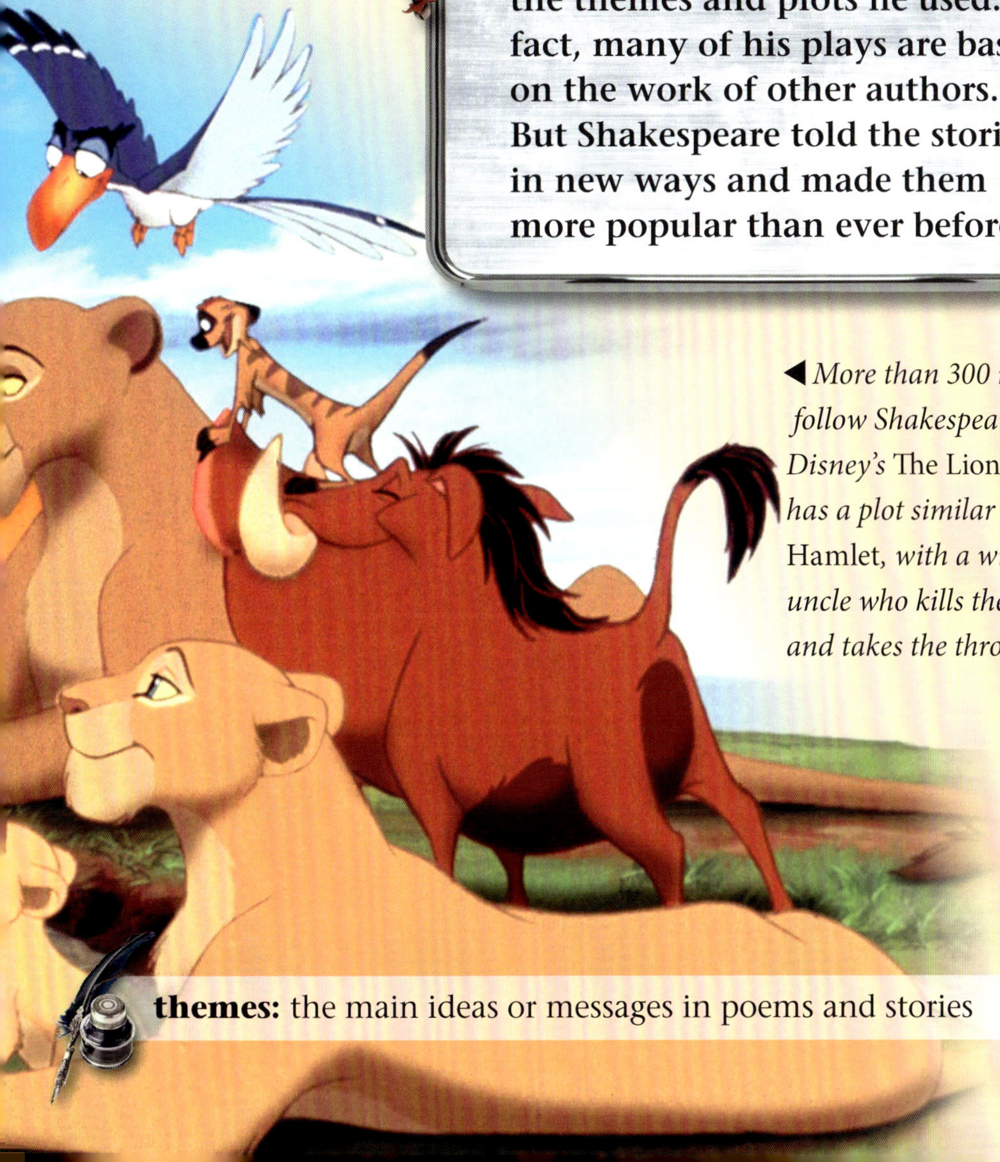

◀ *More than 300 movies follow Shakespeare's plots. Disney's* The Lion King *has a plot similar to* Hamlet, *with a wicked uncle who kills the king and takes the throne.*

themes: the main ideas or messages in poems and stories

Complex Characters

Shakespeare breathed life into characters like no writer had done before. He made them complex and imperfect—like real people. Shakespeare gave voices to the poorest gravediggers, the greatest kings, and everyone in between. They spoke their troubled thoughts aloud. They used powerful poetry and spoke memorable lines that are still quoted today.

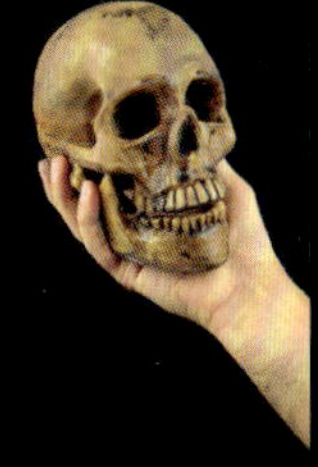

Strong Women

Shakespeare also gave a voice to women—even if they could not speak on stage! At the time, women had little power in society. But Shakespeare featured strong female characters in his plays. Lady Macbeth is a powerful woman who convinces her husband to kill the king. Cleopatra rules Egypt and captures the heart of Mark Antony. Juliet defies her family and chooses her own **fate**.

◀ *Lady Macbeth convinces her husband to commit murder, but she later goes mad and dies.*

"To be, or not to be,—that is the question."

This line from *Hamlet* is one of the most famous ever written. It is part of a long soliloquy in which Hamlet considers killing himself.

fate: the course of someone's life, often seen as beyond their control

▲ Shakespeare invented words when he needed them for his poems and plays.

A Play on Words

Shakespeare invented thousands of words in the English language. There were no English grammar rules or dictionaries at the time. The country was growing fast and the language was changing constantly. Shakespeare borrowed words from ancient books and foreign languages. He also changed and joined English words in new ways.

Here are some of the words Shakespeare invented that we still use today: arch-villain, bedazzled, belongings, bloody, bump, cold-blooded, dawn, eventful, eyeball, fashionable, generous, gloomy, gossip, hurry, leaky, lonely, luggage, majestic, manager, mimic, moonbeam, schoolboy, scuffle, swagger, uncomfortable, unreal, and zany.

Shakespeare's Sayings

Some lines from Shakespeare's plays have become sayings over time. Sayings are short, well-known statements that are used often. They use **figurative language** to paint pictures with words. Some of the sayings Shakespeare invented are: household words, elbow room, break the ice, heart of gold, in a pickle, dead as a doornail, love is blind, wild-goose chase, and brave new world.

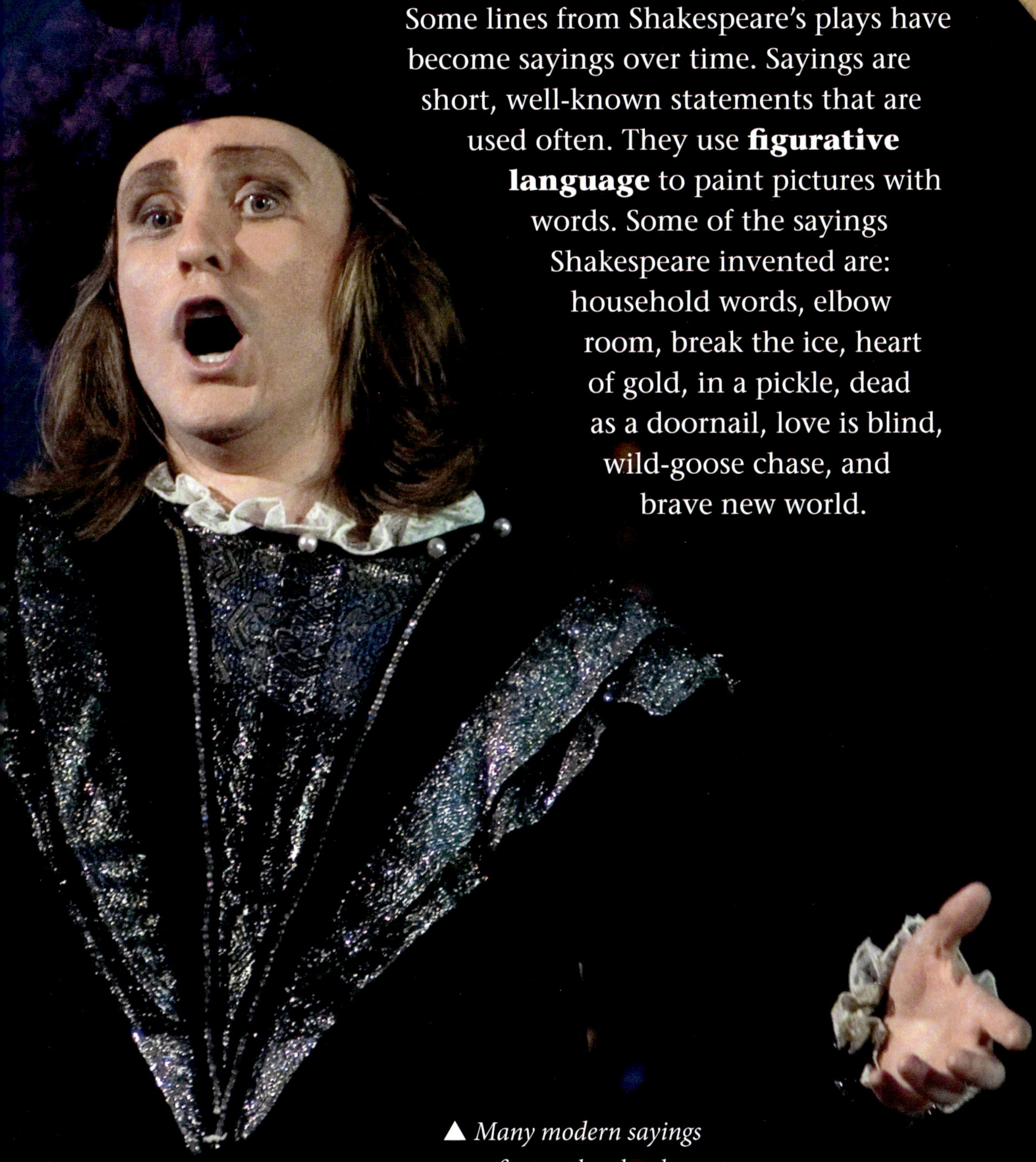

▲ *Many modern sayings were first spoken by characters in Shakespeare's plays.*

figurative language: words that do not have their usual meanings

Break a Leg!

Shakespeare wrote plays to entertain audiences in a local theater. Today, he continues to delight crowds around the world. Shakespeare's plays are performed more than any other playwright's. Renaissance fairs and **festivals** celebrate his life and times. The English town of Stratford-upon-Avon draws millions of visitors each year.

▼ *Each week, Shakespeare's plays are performed on stages around the world.*

Best Seller

William Shakespeare is one of the best-selling authors of all time. His work has sold more than four billion copies around the world. His poems and plays have been translated into nearly every known language—including sign language and Klingon! Klingon is a fictional language spoken in the *Star Trek* television series and movies.

▲ *Shakespeare's plays have been published in thousands of different editions for nearly 400 years.*

The Stratford Festival is an annual celebration of Shakespeare's plays. Held in the Canadian city of Stratford, Ontario, it draws hundreds of thousands of visitors each year. They attend plays and concerts and learn all about the Swan of Avon.

festivals: organized events with plays, music, or other activities

Bringing the House Down

One of Shakespeare's greatest **legacies** is the Globe theater. He helped build it in 1599, and his popular plays helped fill it with people. The Globe was one of the biggest and best theaters in London. But in 1613, a special-effects cannon misfired during a performance of *Henry VIII*. The roof of the Globe caught fire and the theater burned to the ground.

Around the Globe

Shakespeare and other sharers rebuilt the Globe in the same spot the next year. The theater stayed open until 1642. Then it was closed and later pulled down by a ruler named Oliver Cromwell. Cromwell did not approve of plays, music, or other forms of entertainment. In 1997, a theater called Shakespeare's Globe was built near the site of the original theater. Researchers used drawings and stories to carefully recreate the famous playhouse.

▼ *Today, the modern Globe draws Shakespeare fans from around the globe.*

"He was not of an age, but for all time!"

Fellow playwright Ben Jonson, describing the life and work of William Shakespeare

legacies: important things passed down to others

Learning More

Books

Graphic Shakespeare
by Penny Clarke, Michael Ford, *et al*
(Scribo, 2015)

Shakespeare (DK Eyewitness Books)
by DK Publishing
(DK Children, 2015)

Tales from Shakespeare
by Charles and Mary Lamb
(Head and Heart, 2014)

William Shakespeare: His Life and Times (Historical Notebooks)
by Kristen McDermott and Ari Berk (Templar, 2010)

Will's Words: How William Shakespeare Changed the Way You Talk
by Jane Sutcliffe
(Charlesbridge, 2016)

Websites

www.bbc.co.uk/schools/primaryhistory/famouspeople/william_shakespeare/
The BBC Primary History: William Shakespeare.

www.shakespearesglobe.com/playground/exploring-shakespeare
Shakespeare's Globe: Exploring Shakespeare.

www.laits.utexas.edu/shakespearekids/winedale/globe.html
The University of Texas at Austin: Do Your Own Shakespeare.

www.shakespearesglobe.com/playground
Shakespeare's Globe: The Globe Playground.

www.tvokids.com/games/playingshakespeare
TVOKids: Playing Shakespeare.

Glossary

ado Fuss or foolish talk

amphitheater A round building with layers of seats around a stage

ancient Very old

bubonic plague A deadly disease spread by fleas

dynasty A line of rulers from a particular family

fate The course of someone's life, often seen as beyond their control

festivals Organized events with plays, music, or other activities

feuding Long, bitter fighting between families

figurative language Words that do not have their usual meanings

legacies Important things passed down to others

literature Written works that are considered very good or important

opportunity A good chance to succeed

playwright Someone who writes plays

reign A period in which a king or queen rules

relevant Meaningful in today's world

romances Stories that blend comedy, tragedy, and magic

soliloquies Speeches that show the thoughts of lone characters

syllable One part of a word, which takes one "beat"

themes The main ideas or messages in poems and stories

tragedies Stories with sad events and unhappy endings

upstart Rising to power or fame quickly

Index

Entries in **bold** refer to pictures

acting 6, 12, 15
Antony and Cleopatra 39
As You Like It 6
Bacon, Sir Francis 33, **33**

birth 8, **8**, 9
brothers and sisters 9

characters **6–7**, 16, 17, 18, 20, 22, 30, 31, 35, 36, 37, 38
children 11, 23
comedies 16–17, 31
Cromwell, Oliver 45

death 34, 35

education 10, 29, 32
Elizabeth I 13, **13**, 15, **20–21**, 21

festivals 42, 43
First Folio 34, **34**

Globe, the **14–15**, 15, 28, 31, 44, 45
Greene, Robert 29

Hamlet 23, **31**, 39
Hathaway, Anne 11, **11**, 35
Henry VI 13, 21
Henry VIII 44
histories 13, 20–21

James I 15, 26
Jonson, Ben 30, 45

King Lear 23, **23**
King's Men 15

language 5, 35, 40–41, 43
London 8, 12, 13, 16, 18, 20, 28, 44
Lord Chamberlain's Men 14

Macbeth **22**, 23, **38–39**, 39
Marlowe, Christopher 30, 33
Midsummer Night's Dream, A 14, **17**

parents 8, 9, 11
plague 16, **16**, 18
plots 16, 31, 35, 37
poems 5, 7, 18, 19, 35, 43
printing press 10

quartos 34
quill 5, **5**

"Rape of Lucrece" 18
Renaissance 9, 22, 30, 42
Richard III 21
romances 26, 27
Romeo and Juliet 14, **24–25**, 25, 39

Shakespeare's Globe **44–45**, 45
sharers 15, 45
soliloquies 31, 39
sonnets 19, **19**
special effects 27, **27**
Stratford-upon-Avon 8, **8**, **9**, 28, **28–29**, 29, **35**, 42

The Tempest **26**
The Two Gentlemen of Verona **20–21**
Theatre, The 14
themes 36, 37
tragedies 22–23, 24, 31

"Venus and Adonis" 18, **18**

women 39